But ask the animals,
teach you, or the bir
ama they will tell
to the earth, and
or let the fish

a season of
Rejoicing

...a season of

Rejoicing

ELIZABETH M. HOEKSTRA

WITH THE WATERCOLORS OF MARLENE McLOUGHLIN

CROSSWAY BOOKS • WHEATON, ILLINOIS
A DIVISION OF GOOD NEWS PUBLISHERS

A Season of Rejoicing

Copyright © 2000 by Elizabeth M.Hoekstra

Published by Crossway Books
    a division of Good News Publishers
    1300 Crescent Street
    Wheaton, Illinois 60187

Cover and interior illustrations: Marlene McLoughlin

Book Design: Liita Forsyth

Hand-tooled leather for cover: Bob Roberts

First printing 2000

Printed in the United States of America

Library of Congress Cataloging-in-Publication Data

Hoekstra, Elizabeth M. 1962-
 A season of rejoicing / Elizabeth M. Hoekstra.
  p. cm. (All creation sings)
 ISBN 1-58134-206-3 (alk. paper)
 1. Meditations. 2. Summer—Religious aspects—Christianity—Meditations.
I. Title.
BV4832.2.H596 2000
242—dc21

                   00-009048
                     CIP

15	14	13	12	11	10	09	08	07	06	05	04	03	02	01	00
15	14	13	12	11	10	9	8	7	6	5	4	3	2	1	

Dedication

To my sisters,
Melinda and Mandy,
who inspire me and my garden to fuller growth
and to Christen, my sister in Christ

The following meditations on the parallels between the Creator and His creation stem from the experiences of our family on our small New Hampshire farm. With these words, I've invited you into our home, our garden, our barn, and our land. I hope you are encouraged by my transparency, along with that of my children, Geneva and Jordan, and my husband, Peter. My prayer is that you'll find in your own life reflections of the weeding, repairing, planting, growing, and renovations that the Lord works in everyone who belongs to Him.

Come Grow with Us

ASK THE ANIMALS, and they will teach you, or the birds of the air, and they will tell you; or speak to the earth, and it will teach you, or let the fish of the sea inform you. Which of these does not know that the hand of the Lord has done this? In his hand is the life of every creature and the breath of all mankind.

Job 12:7-10

The Lord Is Mighty

God is mighty ... and firm in his purpose.

JOB 36:5

A Map for Our Lives

Your word is a lamp to my feet and a light for my path.

PSALM 119:105

AN ICE CAP once crept across what are now the New England states, smoothing jagged hills, carving valleys, and carrying stones. The glaciers in the valleys deposited granite boulders. The valleys filled with glacier water and rain. Thus, a glacier lake was born.

One might think that a glacier lake has a uniform sloping shelf in the middle. But one of the characteristics of a glacier lake is the presence of rocks—lots of them. Glaciers usually were indiscriminate about where the boulders they carried along landed on the floor of the valleys. Some piled up right in the middle of an otherwise wide-open valley. Consequently, most of the lakes across New England cannot be safely navigated without a map—a very detailed map—pinpointing the rocks and boulders.

Do you see the similarity between glacier lakes and our lives? We too need a detailed map of the rocky spots we might hit during our lives. Some of these rocky spots are called temptations. Just like uninformed boaters without a map, sometimes we cruise along oblivious to the sharp rocks that lie under the surface waiting to rip a hole in our hulls. Where can we get a map to help us avoid those lurking rocks?

God's Word is our lake map. The Proverbs remind us of the pitfalls of human nature. The Old Testament cautions us on the jagged-edged consequences of repeated sins. Many of the Psalms tell us of God's tender guiding hand through rocky spots, while the New Testament confirms our future hope of a safe passage.

Won't you take hold of the map of God's Word and allow it to guide you safely past the rocks and boulders of your life?

MORE SCRIPTURE FOR STUDY:
Psalm 119:129-133; Proverbs 11:14;
John 16:12-13; Colossians 3:16-17

The Lord's Communication

That you may love the LORD your God, listen to his voice,
and hold fast to him.

DEUTERONOMY 30:20a

MY GRANDFATHER ALWAYS SAID that he felt closer to the Lord while on his knees weeding the garden than in church. He felt God's life-giving presence with warm earth under his knees and dirt-smudged hands. He and his brother had a "friendly competition" (as my grandmother called it) as to who could have peas on the table first in the summer— preferably before July 4. This was not easy in his home state of Massachusetts!

My grandfather worked hard tending his garden and never seemed short of the life lessons available there. He learned that the Lord can meet you wherever you are. The Lord met my grandfather in his garden.

Since God created you with passions and gifts, of course He'll know where to find you. One of the ways He communicates with us is through the very gifts He's given us. Those gifts are an open line of communication to Him. Where is your heart? Do you have a passion to teach? A desire to spread the Gospel?

A heart for the injured or ill? Or, perhaps like my grandfather, you want to nurture and grow new life. Whatever helps you feel fulfilled is a gift from the Lord that allows you to feel His ministering touch.

I know I feel and hear Him the most when I'm tending my animals. It's as if the Lord and I have a special language that I can perceive in the nurture of my pets. (I think Noah had the same language!) The Lord gave me the desire and aptitude to care for animals. So why wouldn't He use that same avenue to communicate to me? It's an established thread right to my heart.

Watch for ways in which the Lord communicates to you through your areas of giftedness. Maybe He communicates through the soft touch of a child you're teaching. Maybe He communicates while you're on the golf course surrounded by nature. He will be faithful to reveal Himself to you in the place where you can hear Him best.

MORE SCRIPTURE FOR STUDY:
Deuteronomy 4:35-40; Psalm 19:1-4;
John 10:27; Hebrews 4:7, 12-13

Land of the Free

*The land on which your feet have walked will be your inheritance
and that of your children forever, because you have
followed the LORD wholeheartedly.*

JOSHUA 14:9

OUR COUNTRY WAS founded on the principle of independence. The Puritans and Separatists boldly broke away from the legalism of the Church of England to be free to worship the Lord on their own terms and on their own *ground*—the very ground upon which you and I stand. They didn't seek freedom as an act of defiance. Rather, they felt called to worship God with total abandon, without restraint from a governing body. But what started as a peaceable move turned into a bloody war based on power, greed, and jealousy.

Since I live on the East Coast, I've visited the places where battles raged, blood flowed into the earth, and good men's souls departed, alone and far, far from home. These men *believed* in what they fought for, believed that their lives mattered, believed that their land mattered. They had a vast vision for their children, their grandchildren, and their great-grandchildren: freedom.

Have you thought about the fact that the land around you was prayed for, fought for, and died for? We live in a Promised Land of sorts—a land built on the promises of God. I can imagine the Pilgrims—then the colonists and later the patriots—claiming verses from the Bible to steady themselves during times of doubt. "He will make your righteousness shine like the dawn, the justice of your cause like the noonday sun. . . . For evil men will be cut off, but those who hope in the LORD will inherit the land" (Ps. 37:6-9).

Do we treasure that same confidence about the land we live in? This land is an answer to God's promise. Will you treasure the privilege of freedom for which many of our ancestors fought? Will you follow in their footsteps and worship the Lord in the freedom we are guaranteed under the Constitution?

Over the coming days, reflect on the freedoms you have as an American citizen and as a child in the family of God. As you take a walk, say a prayer of thanks for the Christian principles on which your feet and heart stand.

MORE SCRIPTURE FOR STUDY:
Psalms 40:2; 119:32; Galatians 5:1;
Ephesians 2:19-22

Thankful for Differences

You will not take pride in one man over against another.
For who makes you different from anyone else?

1 CORINTHIANS 4:6b-7a

PETER AND I stood on the shore of the Atlantic Ocean. The sand warmed our bare feet, but the surf rolled in to cool them.

I squinted against the sun, my eyes sweeping the far horizon and seeing only inviting blue water and a few distant boats. I turned to tell Peter how beautiful it looked; how the peaceful and mesmerizing lull of the empty sea drew me to the water's edge. But I saw that Peter's back was to the water and me. He stood alert, watching a party crowd and a volleyball game down the beach a stretch. I thought, *How can you watch* people *when this great expanse of water beckons?* But then I realized how this scene painted a defining picture of our differences. I love open spaces, water, and privacy. He loves people, activity, and sports.

How like the Lord to put two diametrically opposed people together! Have you found that to be true in your life too? Why does He couple us with people so different from us? For a number of reasons: to teach us tolerance; to help us mature; to lessen our self-centeredness.

As we accept other people's differences, we become more Christlike. Jesus has no bias, no personality preferences. He loves all people alike, despite their differences. While on earth He even called the hard-working, undoubtedly smelly fishermen to be His disciples. I'm not sure I'd want to hang out with a bunch of guys fresh off a fishing boat. But Jesus did. He looked beyond their differences.

Can you also look beyond the differences of those around you and—taking that a step further—be appreciative about those differences? My husband and I differ in complementary ways. Because of our varied outlooks our children are growing up with a well-rounded view of the world around them. Can you find a way to be grateful for the differences of the people in your life?

MORE SCRIPTURE FOR STUDY:
1 Corinthians 12:4-13; 15:39-44

Deep Roots

Blessed is the man ... [whose] delight is in the law of the LORD....
He is like a tree planted by streams of water, which yields its fruit
in season and whose leaf does not wither.

PSALM 1:1-3a

WE LIVE AT THE top of a natural watershed. Our land has a bowl shape with our house on one lip and fields and woods on the other. The center of our property drops down into a swamp. In the spring, the runoff from the hillsides turns the swamp into a brown, muddy pool. A stream runs through the center of the swamp, making its way to a bigger stream across another valley. As spring turns to summer, the swamp recedes and the edges of the water take on a green fluorescent sheen from the growth of bacteria.

We had a drought one summer, as all places do at some time or another. The fields turned brown; the grass was as crisp as cut and dried hay. The swamp pulled into itself more and more, exposing mud, rotting leaves, and twigs. The stream no longer had enough height to climb over the lip into the culvert. The swamp began to stagnate, which caused it to stink.

Not surprisingly, the evergreens and deciduous trees around the swamp stayed a glorious green. But the farther the tree, plant, or shrub was from the swamp, the more withered it looked. Only the oldest trees with the deepest roots could weather the drought. Yet while the swamp seemed to rot, the springs underneath kept the trees alive.

Let's face it—being a Christian is hard sometimes. Seasons of little refreshment come. At times I feel dry, cracked, and seem to stink from my own rot! How about you? What's underneath the stagnation? Has the truth of God's nourishing, ever-present, living water changed? Are we trying to live off the surface rot and mud, or are we remembering to send our roots deeper and deeper?

Trees instinctually send their roots down. We have to make a conscious choice, however, to do so. Will you be willing with me to persevere even in drought? "For if the willingness is there, the gift is acceptable according to what one has, not according to what he does not have" (2 Cor. 8:12).

This week, send your roots deeper in the Lord and His promises. Even if you're not experiencing a spiritual drought, concentrate on establishing a root system with the Lord that will not dry up. "The root of the righteous flourishes" (Prov. 12:12b).

MORE SCRIPTURE FOR STUDY:
Psalms 51:12; 91:15-16; Hebrews 6:18-19;
1 Peter 5:10

The Lure of Garbage

Do not love the world or anything in the world....
The world and its desires pass away.

1 JOHN 1:15-17a

OUR FOUR-YEAR-OLD DOG, Gibraltar, is a garbage dog. She'll sneak to the trash cans or bags and gorge herself on rotting food, torn wrappers, and tissues if the bags aren't secure and she's not discovered. I've found her surrounded by picked-over fruit peels, scattered coffee grounds, and shredded bags. She'll drop her eyes, sheepishly wag her tail, and grin as if to say, "I know this was wrong, but I had such a *great* time!"

What I can't seem to get her to understand is the cause and effect of eating garbage. Inevitably she gets a swollen belly and tummy cramps. She'll stretch out on the floor and moan, trying to relieve the pain. (She *is* a little dramatic.) Her mournful eyes seem to ask, "Isn't there something you can do to help me?" No, there isn't, especially since it was her choice to eat the garbage. But once she's better in a few hours or days, I know she'll go right back to the trash cans.

Maybe she doesn't have the cognitive ability to grasp the simple concept: eat trash, get sick. But are we any better? Don't we just as readily gorge ourselves on the garbage of the world? Then, feeling sick with sin, we call out to the Lord, "Isn't there something You can do to get me out of this pain?" Like my dog, we're often slow learners. We need a remedial class in the cause and effect of garbage consumption.

What is the "garbage pile" in your life? What leaves you feeling sick and lethargic? Maybe it's the consumption of less-than-wholesome TV programs or magazines. Perhaps it's an attitude such as pride or deceit. Or, could it literally be overeating? Make a decision today to ask the Lord to give you the strength to avoid visiting this tempting garbage site. See how much healthier you will feel tomorrow!

MORE SCRIPTURE FOR STUDY:
Proverbs 3:1-8; 28:7; Matthew 9:9-13;
1 Corinthians 10:11-13

Our Rock

On this rock I will build my church, and the gates of Hades will not overcome it.

MATTHEW 16:18

IMAGINE BOARDING A marginally safe sailing craft. The smell of repair tar stings your nostrils. As soon as the biceps-thick line is released, the sails are raised and the wind blows against the straining patched canvas. Land melts behind the stern. Nothing but belly-churning swells meet the bow. Five weeks later, with muscles weak from inactivity in the hold and ears ringing from the relentless pounding of water mere inches from your restless head, you hear word of land ahead. The anchor splashes. A few passengers clamber into a rowboat, anxious to reach the shore. You hear whispers of prayers: *Is this the place? Is this where we should begin, Lord?* You gingerly step off the little craft and onto a rock. *Yes, this is it.*

Do you recognize this as the landing of the Pilgrims? Historians can only guess which rock is the "real" Plymouth Rock. Yet a good-sized rock on the water's edge in Plymouth, Rhode Island, is enshrined as the original rock that received the feet of the freedom-searching Pilgrims.

If it had been me—and perhaps you have a similar thought—my first words of thanks for a safe passage and to claim the New World for Christ might have been Jesus' words: "On this rock I will build my church."

To me that one rock has a double impact. It represents the unswerving determination of the Pilgrims to seek a new life in a new land with the freedom to establish churches in the name of the Lord Jesus Christ. The rock also represents Christ Himself. He is immovable, solid, and steadfast—a strong and safe "place" on which to stand. "The LORD is my rock, my fortress, and my deliverer; my God is my rock, in whom I take refuge" (Ps. 18:2a). That Rock is personal, isn't it?

Do you have a Plymouth Rock in your life: a place where you landed and knew that new life was coming; someplace where you felt Christ's protection and security? If you have had this kind of experience, relive it by writing about it in a journal or by telling it to a friend. If you're feeling wind-tossed and aimless, ask the Lord to guide you to your own Plymouth Rock. He will land you safely and establish His kingdom within you.

MORE SCRIPTURE FOR STUDY:
2 Samuel 22:1-7; Psalm 61:2; Isaiah 26:1-4;
Matthew 7:24-27

Planted to Grow

The sun rises with scorching heat and withers the plant....
Blessed is the man who perseveres under trial.

JAMES 1:11-12a

THE SUN IS indiscriminate with its rays and heat. It doesn't choose which plants will thrive in its scorching light and which plants will die of sunburn and thirst. The discrimination belongs to the gardener, not the sun. Gardeners with green thumbs pick and plant bushes and flowers that will rejoice in the sun. They know which ones will shrink and die in the sun. They know that a rosebush won't thrive in a shadowed, dense thicket.

What a travesty when we try to force a shade-desiring plant into all-day sun. Think about it: in the wild a plant won't naturally grow in a place where it is sure to die, will it? Doing so would be against its nature.

By the same token, the Lord won't plant us someplace where we are bound to wither. He's a discriminating gardener—careful to nestle His tender plants in the soil they need with the right amount of water and the correct amount of sun exposure. He gently prunes and weeds around the roots, nurturing strong, healthy plants.

Would a good gardener plant pumpkin seeds in sandy soil or peas in heavy clay? No! He or she wants the ensuing plants to succeed. So it is with the Lord. He wants us to grow and bear fruit. He may test our roots during the temporary drought of unconfessed sin. Or He may prune the useless and burdensome branches of bad attitudes or self-centeredness from our hearts. But He will not sever our stalks or tear us out by the roots. Why? He knows He can grow a plentiful harvest in us right where He's planted us.

Have you wondered whether or not you're in the right part of God's garden? Will you take hold of the assurance that the Lord has planted you in the right place in which to grow and produce a harvest?

MORE SCRIPTURE FOR STUDY:
Matthew 13:1-8, 18-23; John 15:1-8;
1 Corinthians 10:11-13

Positive Effects

You became imitators of us and of the Lord....
And so you became a model to all the believers....
Your faith in God has become known everywhere.

1 THESSALONIANS 1:6-8

DURING HOT SUMMER weekends my family and I can be found swimming or sunning on our boat anchored in a lake half a mile from our home. Sometimes we'll cruise the lake, the wind cooling and drying our skin. Other times we'll drift and watch boats skim by, boats that often pull water-skiers or water-tubers behind them. Their passing stirs up waves that causes us to pitch for a few minutes. But the boater who caused the swells is long gone around a bend, into a cove, or past the central island.

This reminds me so much of our faith. For good or ill we affect others by our words or actions. Sometimes we minister to someone and are long gone before we even see how our actions affected that person's life. I call that a *ripple-effect faith.*

The ripples of our faith are really twofold. First, we have faith that the opportunities the Lord places in our path for ministry will cause a ripple in someone's life. Second, as the Scripture above notes, our model of a faithful life hopefully will ripple into the subconscious of others.

When Peter and I were first married, we led the junior high youth group of our church. We enjoyed ministering to the kids, answering their tough questions, and rejoicing with them when they moved on to the senior high group. Those young people are now adults with their own children, jobs, and faith walks. Although they are scattered from their original home church, we hear about them from their parents. Almost all of them at one point or another have commented on how Peter and I modeled Christianity to them. That's humbling. But even more sobering is the fact that three of them have died.

Therein is the seriousness of ripple-effect faith. We can't know the immediacy of the need for a faith model in others' lives. Be assured though—the need is there. Take a look at your life in the coming weeks. Whom are you influencing? What ripple of faith are you creating through your faith walk? Will you prayerfully look for situations where your faith can be a model for others?

MORE SCRIPTURE FOR STUDY:
Proverbs 3:3; Colossians 4:2-6; Philemon 4-7;
1 Peter 4:7-11

Negative Effects

You became imitators of us and of the Lord ....
And so you became a model to all the believers ....
Your faith in God has become known everywhere.

1 THESSALONIANS 1:6-8

BELIEVE IT OR NOT, our faith walks can have a negative ripple effect at times. I'm reminded of a Sunday afternoon family outing on our motorboat. We blithely dashed along at seventeen knots (about twenty miles per hour) or so. Going around a corner, we passed a canoe with four people in it before we even had a chance to slow down. I desperately wanted to reclaim the waves we caused as I saw their weighted craft bob, turn sideways, and take on water. We had two choices: ignore what we'd done and continue on our way or turn around (slowly!) and offer our apologies. In the seconds it took to reduce the throttle and make the choice, we realized that we knew the group of canoers. Sheepishly, we crept up next to them, apologized, and took one of them on board to transport to shore.

What if we hadn't known them? It would have been easy to just keep going and not look back. Sound familiar? How often in our spiritual lives do we swamp others and continue on our merry way, not realizing or acknowledging the damage we've left in our wake? These negative ripples can include a judgmental or self-righteous attitude. I know I've sometimes allowed a wave of anger to break over my spouse. At other times I've damaged someone else's feelings in swollen pride.

How about you? Is your personality like a speedboat on a small lake—sending damaging swells over people as you cruise through life? If so, think about slowing down and taking a careful look around at the ripples your faith are causing. Are they about to swamp someone? Will the ripples you leave encourage others to follow your path—a path of righteousness that leads to the Lord? What kind of faith wake do you want to leave?

MORE SCRIPTURE FOR STUDY:
Deuteronomy 6:1-8; Psalm 145:3-7;
2 Thessalonians 2:13-17

Sonlight

And I—in righteousness I will see your face; when I awake,
I will be satisfied with seeing your likeness.

PSALM 17:15

FOR TWO WEEKS on a lake in central New Hampshire, I wake each morning to the first rays of a July sun fingering across the windowsill next to my head. As I feel its warmth brush my face, I roll over and watch it push the darkness from the trees on the other side of the muted cove, filtering light clear to the heavens and masking the last stars. *This* is my vacation—waking at dawn to witness God's daily reminder of light overcoming darkness.

He created the sun as a representation of Himself. Although we won't see Him until we reach heaven, He's given us clues to His characteristics in all of creation. David so eloquently describes a longing to see God in the above verse from Psalm 17: "When I awake, I will be satisfied with seeing your likeness."

The sun is a vivid representation of God. Darkness cannot dwell with light; light will scatter it every time. It highlights a clear path and illuminates rocks and roots. It always shines, even at night on the other side of the world and above gloomy clouds. Its rays nourish new growth. It will never be consumed or depleted.

Now reread the above paragraph and insert the Lord's name instead of the word *it*. This is what David was thinking!

Today, even if the day is overcast, offer praise to the Lord for giving us senses to help us understand how He is represented by the sun. "Let the light of your face shine upon us, O LORD" (Ps. 4:6b).

MORE SCRIPTURE FOR STUDY:
Deuteronomy 7:8-9; Psalm 111;
Revelation 1:12-16

The Lord Is a Rock

The LORD is the rock eternal.

ISAIAH 26:4

Heaven-Directed Hope

*Blessed is he whose help is the God of Jacob, whose hope is in
the LORD his God, the Maker of heaven and earth.*

PSALM 146:5-6a

UP AND DOWN the East Coast in the 1700-1800s, seafarers' wives watched for their men to return from the unforgiving sea. Sea captains' houses clung to the high, rocky points along the shore. Their sturdy frames were tall with open decks on the top floor for an unhindered view of the sea. Women walked these decks day and night searching the horizon and wearing down the floor-boards until they were shiny and concave. These decks weren't called "widow walks" for nothing. Years went by with the ever-hopeful women waiting and waiting and waiting.

Did pacing get these women anywhere? No. Did worry provide them with energy for all of the other tasks of being a sea captain's wife? No. Did their anxiety bring their men home sooner? No. Did the men always return from the sea? No. Yet never hearing word either way, the women could not get on with their lives. They stayed in forced limbo, always hopeful, always disappointed.

Do we ever find ourselves in a similar place? Our spirits restlessly pace and wait, hopeful for some return on a promise. The prophet Isaiah tells us that our hope needs to rest in God, not in man. "You will know that I am the Lord; those who hope in me will not be disappointed" (49:23). When our feet are rooted to the Lord —not restlessly pacing in our own strength—He will not disappoint us.

Are there areas in your life where your hope is directed toward events or others instead of to the Lord? Perhaps you're hoping to become pregnant, searching for a job, waiting for physical health, or feeling anxious about your child. Can you release those anxieties and put your hope squarely in the Lord's hands? Pray with me:

> *Here, Lord. Take these desires of my heart.*
> *You know what's best for me,*
> *what the best timing is, what the best route is.*
> *I'll trust You not to disappoint me.*

MORE SCRIPTURE FOR STUDY:
Psalm 33:12-22; Isaiah 40:31;
Jeremiah 29:11; 1 Peter 3:12-15

Thirst Quenchers

Even the wild animals pant for you; the streams of water have dried up and fire has devoured the open pastures.

JOEL 1:20

ANIMALS CAN LITERALLY die of thirst in a matter of hours. Horses in particular are susceptible to dehydration and a malady called colic. Because horses are grazing animals, their digestive systems are always on the move. But they need to drink water constantly to lubricate the passage of grass or hay through their systems. Without water their intestines become impacted, gas builds, and pain rocks them to their knees. If left untreated, their intestines rupture—all for lack of water.

I lost a black horse on a hot day to colic. She wasn't completely out of water when I found her rolling in pain in her stall. But she had passed the threshold of wanting a drink. She panted, thrashed, and kicked at her swollen belly. The veterinarian treated her with every imaginable remedy. Nothing worked. She died and I cried.

Dehydration is an insidious condition. The saying goes that if you're thirsty, you're already dehydrated. The solution lies in prevention: drink before you get thirsty.

Isn't that true in our spiritual walks? Isn't it easy to continue our busy pace and neglect a needed break for the thirst-quenching living water—Jesus Christ? It seems we are especially susceptible to spiritual dehydration in the summer months when relaxed schedules and vacation days beckon. But what will happen if we wait too long to replenish the living water in our bodies? Like the horse, we'll find ourselves panting, dried out, and in need of water to relieve our discomfort.

Isaiah 55:1a says, "Come, all you who are thirsty, come to the waters." The discomfort of spiritual thirst—feeling dry or fatigued in our spirits— reminds us to return to the Lord to drink His living water. Jesus is our solution for eternal spiritual thirst. Pointing to a dipper of well water He said, "Everyone who drinks this water will be thirsty again, but whoever drinks the water I give him will never thirst" (John 4:13-14a).

Take a drink.

MORE SCRIPTURE FOR STUDY:
Psalms 36:9; 107:9; John 4:1-26;
Revelation 21:6

A Tempting Offer

*Pay attention to my wisdom … that you may maintain
discretion and your lips may preserve knowledge.
For the lips of an adulteress drip honey, and
her speech is smoother than oil.*

PROVERBS 5:1-3

SHE STOOD CLEAN and sleek with beautiful molded curves. She carried
our dreams right on deck. I could see our family on this cruising boat. I envisioned starry nights, our anchor hooked securely underwater and a gentle
breeze rocking us to sleep in the quarters below deck. I imagined our family
smiling and tanned, iced drinks in hand, trolling the waters of the Atlantic or
large lakes in New England. Oh, she was a seductress all right—sweet in her
appearance and whispering, "I can be yours, I can be yours."

The problem was that Peter and I had made a decision to work toward
paying off our debts. We wanted to be free from car payments and free from
his business debts. From study, talks, and prayer, we knew this was a wise and
godly decision. But oh, that boat . . .

Most Americans live well beyond their means. We all suffer from the instant gratification pattern of "buy now, worry about payments later." With us, it seemed as if the devil weaseled his way in right when we'd made a righteous commitment. He knows how to undermine willpower with tempting offers.

Has the devil made you an offer that you need to refuse? If so, stick to your commitment. You might make your commitment verbal and written. For example, you might carry a note to yourself in your pocket. Your commitment offered in the Lord's name will always overpower a whisper of temptation from the devil. Try it.

By the way, we didn't buy the boat.

MORE SCRIPTURE FOR STUDY:
Matthew 4:1-11; 1 Corinthians 10:13; 2 Corinthians 4:18; Philippians 4:8-9

Refreshing Sonlight

*[The sun] rises at one end of the heavens and makes its circuit to
the other; nothing is hidden from its heat.*

PSALM 19:6

HEAT WAVES. They are called waves because they swell and wash over you
with no reprieve or relief. You feel as though you can't breathe. Your body
feels limp and wringing wet. Your mouth feels full of chalk dust. You're anxious for a refreshing drink. Your senses become muddled. During a blistering
heat wave, "nothing is hidden from [the sun's] heat," as David said.

What else do we associate with the word *heat*? Pressure? Police officers?
Tension and demand? *Heat* is used to describe tense circumstances when people are forced into situations of decision making or compromise. Are you feeling the "heat" in an area of your life right now? Are there relationships that
threaten to burn you? Are you faced with a job complication that is forcing
you to make a hurried decision?

I know I feel the heat the most when there are too many demands on my day. My checklists don't have enough check marks next to them. I start pressuring myself to perform beyond what I am physically capable of doing.

With heat in our lives, we become desperate for a break—something to relieve the pressure and cool our senses. We search for a shady spot to rest and regain strength before we push on again. The reprieve comes in the form of the Son—God's Son, Jesus Christ. Sonlight isn't too hot. It doesn't leave us desperate. Instead it acts as a coolant, refreshing our inner souls.

"The LORD will guide you always; he will satisfy your needs in a sun-scorched land and will strengthen your frame. You will be like a well-watered garden, like a spring whose waters never fail" (Isa. 58:11). That's reassurance you can recite with confidence during a scorching heat wave! In the coming hot weeks of summer (and at other times in your life), remember to seek a refreshing wave of Sonlight when you feel overwhelmed by heat.

MORE SCRIPTURE FOR STUDY:
Psalm 23:1-3; Acts 3:16-20; 2 Peter 3:8-11

Our Muddy Nature

A sow that is washed goes back to her wallowing in the mud.

2 PETER 2:22b

WE RAISED PIGS only once. I didn't need to ever do it again. At first they were cute—kind of wiggly and squealy with little brown curious eyes. But as pigs are supposed to do, they grew. The bigger they got, the more . . . well . . . piglike they became.

Second to escaping (during which I tracked them down on horseback to chase them back to the barn), wallowing in the mud puddle around their water bucket was their favorite activity. The mud wasn't just dirt and water mixed together. They contributed some choice material to make it really gooey and smelly. By the time they were ready for market—at about 250 pounds—they would threaten me when I would try to clean their water bucket. They would grab hold of my bootlaces and pull hard. They liked their mud and didn't want it cleaned up!

As offensive as they were to my senses, they were just doing what pigs do. They followed their instincts: get good and dirty and stay that way. Getting clean was against their nature. You can take the pig out of the mud, but you can't take the mud out of the pig.

Sound familiar? For us too, staying clean from the dirt in our lives is against our nature. Our nature has the pull of sin. We instinctively gravitate toward the mire of dishonesty, fear, blame, lust, defiance, pride, and rebellion that make us smell pretty bad!

I suspect that David had similar feelings that prompted him to write, "He lifted me out of the slimy pit, out of the mud and the mire; he set my feet on a rock and gave me a firm place to stand" (Ps. 40:2). Even though our nature is to return to sin over and over, the Lord is faithful to repeatedly forgive us. Won't you echo David's prayer and thank Him for giving you a solid place to stand in His name?

MORE SCRIPTURE FOR STUDY:
Luke 15:11-24; 1 Corinthians 15:57-58;
Ephesians 1:7; 1 John 1:9

Giving Back

*Everything comes from you, and we have given you only
what comes from your hand.... O LORD our God,
as for all this abundance ... it comes from your hand,
and all of it belongs to you.*

1 CHRONICLES 29:14b-16

THE PRINCIPLE OF tithing started in the Old Testament when Cain and
Abel offered the Lord the firstfruits of their crops and flocks. It was a test of obedience and discipline to offer the first harvest or the best animal from the
flock to the Lord. After all, the food and animals represented people's liveli-
hood. Whatever they gave away or sacrificed meant less for consumption or
in storage for them.

In the New Testament we find instructions to give from our storehouses
faithfully and cheerfully (2 Cor. 9:7). But in our day of high-rises, fast cars,
and grocery stores what can we give? What are the firstfruits of a twenty-first
century family?

Firstfruits are anything we treasure, anything we hold dear to our hearts.

What comes to mind? Our families, homes, children, money, or time. Why does the Lord instruct us to tithe? For the same reason that the Israelites tithed—as an act of obedience and as a reminder that the Lord desires the best. It's vain of us to believe that these "things" are ours anyway. As the verse above notes, the "abundance" comes from His hand.

But how can we tithe based on things we can't "give away"—like a home or family? We can dedicate what we have as an act of service to the Lord. We can open our homes as places to minister to others. We can teach our children to serve the community. We can give our time to a missions organization or teach Sunday school.

In the days to come, think of a specific way you can tithe. Be sure to act on that decision. You'll be blessed in your act of obedience as you give God your best.

MORE SCRIPTURE FOR STUDY:
Deuteronomy 15:7-11; Malachi 3:6-18;
Acts 20:32-35; Romans 12:6-8

Full Reflection

Those who are wise will shine like the brightness of the heavens,
and those who lead many to righteousness,
like the stars for ever and ever.

DANIEL 12:3

LIVING IN THE country on a dirt road with our closest neighbor about a half mile away allows us to see clear to the heavens. There are so many stars that if you close one eye, you can play connect the dots with your fingertip.

During a clear month, the moon waxes and wanes, receding late in its cycle and then growing stronger and brighter. If the Lord God is represented by the sun around which everything rotates, we can be compared to the moon—a reflection of His light in the darkness.

Like the moon, we go through waxing and waning stages in our faith walks. We all have areas that have the potential for turning us away from the Lord. What areas in your life divert your attention from God? Complacency or defiant sin? Willfulness or a poor heart attitude? When we've turned partially away from the Lord, a smaller portion of His light shines on us. We've regressed to a half-moon or crescent-moon stage—just a tiny slice in the darkness.

In my life complacency stagnates my faith. I feel apathetic about a relationship that needs work. Or I feel defeated about a situation. For example, when a friend hurts my feelings, I resignedly allow the pain to fester. What's happened in each of these scenarios? My faith has waned—my reflected light from the Lord has grown weaker and weaker.

Should we stay in a waning phase? I prefer the opposite cycle—the cycle that turns my face and faith back to the Lord. I want to be perpetually waxing in my faith—drawing closer to the Lord and allowing more of Him to shine in my life. How about you?

MORE SCRIPTURE FOR STUDY:
John 4:1-42; 2 Corinthians 3:12-18

Handpicked

You did not choose me, but I chose you and appointed you to go and bear fruit—fruit that will last.

JOHN 15:16a

ONE OF MY favorite meals to prepare for my family is a roasted chicken—one raised by our own hands—with beans or peas picked from the garden and blueberry muffins made from berries stripped from our highbush patch. Not only does the food taste fresh, clean, and pure, but it satisfies a deeper hunger for self-sufficiency and completion.

It seems that each piece of produce has a story behind it. We reminisce about planting the peas earlier this year than ever before; we talk about the scary snake we saw on the way to the blueberry bushes; we laugh as we remember the chickens' antics during the growing weeks. We savor the collective tastes knowing that each berry or pea pod was handpicked. They seem more tender and precious.

This meal reminds me of how the Lord must feel about each of us as He nurtures our growth and watches the fruit we're producing. Just as my peas are individually handled, so too does the Lord individually handle us.

Jesus tells us, "I have chosen you out of the world" (John 15:19). We've been handpicked to bear spiritual fruit that will nourish others. The Lord takes great delight and satisfaction in bringing us to a full harvest.

Do you feel His handprint upon your life—His invitation for you to be fruitful in His name? Will you accept His nurture?

MORE SCRIPTURE FOR STUDY:
Jeremiah 17:8; Proverbs 11:30;
Matthew 7:15-23; Galatians 5:22-23

Shipwrecked Faith

I give you this instruction in keeping with the prophecies once made about you ... holding on to faith and a good conscience. Some have rejected these and so have shipwrecked their faith.

1 TIMOTHY 1:18-19

SHIPWRECKS LITTER THE waters off the East Coast. Unseen ledges, shoals, rock outcroppings, and sandbars have claimed thousands of boats over the years, from fourteenth-century Spanish galleons to current-day pleasure boats. The sea is unforgiving. An unprepared boat—or even a prepared vessel—can quickly and irrevocably find itself in a desperate situation. The ongoing tally of boats and lives will continue to tick until the end of time.

The imagery of shipwrecked faith is provocative. Storms of fear, confrontation, or grief can push our little vessels of faith onto the rocks. The pounding waves of trials hammer at our crafts. Piece by piece the boat comes apart. First, the hull is smashed; then the topside collapses on itself. Finally, the mast topples and the boat disintegrates. The shipwreck hasn't just stalled the boat's intended passage—it has ended it.

In what areas of your life have you experienced shipwrecked faith? Have you experienced a tragedy? A disappointment? A broken relationship or some other loss? For me the stormy seas of my son's chronic disease threaten my faith. A puff of fear-producing wind pushes my faith craft dangerously close to rocks that can smash my precarious boat.

How can we avoid the jagged rocks that threaten our faith? By renaming our little crafts *Faith* and *Hope*. Two verses from Hebrews explain why. "Faith is being sure of what we hope for and certain of what we do not see" (11:1). If faith is our boat, hope is the anchor that holds us in place and keeps us safe and far away from the faith-smashing rocks. "We have this hope as an anchor for the soul, firm and secure" (6:19a). Hope is the confidence that the current faith-threatening circumstances will be better around the next point of land. It helps us ride out the waves until we can get there.

MORE SCRIPTURE FOR STUDY:
Luke 8:22-25; 1 Corinthians 13:13;
Hebrews 6:16-20; 10:22-23

No Hostages

We were harassed at every turn—conflicts on the outside, fears within.
But God who comforts the downcast, comforted us.

2 CORINTHIANS 7:5-6

OUR LOCAL PONDS and lakes are full of fish, water snakes, and turtles. Some of the turtles have hard shells, triangular heads, and alligator-like tails. They're also big—*really* big. The biggest ones are the snapping turtles. Their shells are easily eighteen inches wide. Their snapping jaws and jagged teeth have been known to drown small dogs or bite off fingers or toes when the turtle was cornered. You don't mess with these cranky, solitary creatures.

One hot day in July my friend and I swam from our anchored boat to a rock thirty feet from shore. As we stroked toward the rock, I caught a quick glimpse of a turtle's tail end slipping into the water. We pulled ourselves up on the rock, taking a breather before swimming back to the boat.

Suddenly I saw the turtle lurking in the shadowed water just a few feet away from the rock on which we sat. I joked to my friend, "I think he's miffed at us for taking his sunning spot." I concluded that as most wild animals are more afraid of humans than we are of them, he would soon swim away. Twenty minutes later, however, he still impatiently swam around the rock, boldly sticking his head out of the water to glare at us. We were held hostage by a snapping turtle!

But were we? He did seem menacing, even harassing. But had we done anything to try to scare him away or, conversely, to provoke him? Neither really. We sat there, surprised by his brazen anger.

How like some of our confrontations with the devil! Do we do anything when he threatens us? Or do we sit in shocked silence and inactivity because he's caught us off-guard? Do we have the authority to tell him to back off? Of course we do! First John 2:14 says, "The word of God lives in you, and you have overcome the evil one." (See also Luke 10:19.) When God lives in us, the threats or harassment from the evil one cannot hinder us. The name of Jesus gives us the authority.

When you feel threatened by the snapping jaws of Satan, tell him, "Get away from me. You cannot hold me hostage by your scare tactics!" Then turn your back and walk confidently away in Christ's name.

MORE SCRIPTURE FOR STUDY:
Psalm 37:27; Isaiah 61:1-3;
Ephesians 6:10-20

Treasure Hunt

In a large house there are articles not only of gold and silver,
but also of wood and clay; some are for noble purposes
and some for ignoble.

2 TIMOTHY 2:20

I WOULD VENTURE to guess that you have each of the elements listed in the above verse. Maybe not the large house part (or maybe you do), but the gold (a wedding band perhaps?), silver (a tea set or your grandmother's silverware?), wood (a serving tray or salad bowl?), and clay (stoneware dishes?).

Some items may feel more valuable to you than others. Although some may not be financially valuable, they have sentimental value. Such attachments are common. We have memories of particular items from our history that inspire us, make us cry, offer us hope, or remind us of promises.

God made us tactile beings. We women in particular have a heightened awareness of our world. He gave us our five senses so that we could experience His creation to the fullest. But have you ever considered that our five senses also can be used to experience Him and His gifts—not material gifts but spiritual gifts?

These gifts are far more valuable than the silver, gold, wood, or clay items we value. They are gifts of God's heart, His mind, His likeness, His knowledge, and His nature. Solomon used a hidden treasure analogy in Proverbs 2:2-5 to describe the search for these attributes of God. As a matter of fact, the verses include some of the five senses in the search for His divine riches!

Who among us does not like a good treasure hunt? At the beach don't we secretly hope to unearth some small treasure? Yet when we read, study, and memorize God's Word, we're on a treasure hunt as we eagerly dig through those nuggets of choice silver and gold. Do we believe those riches are even there for us?

The Lord wants to bestow His finest riches on you this summer. (Actually that's a year-round assurance.) Will you search them out and recognize them as treasures when you've found them? Take time to reflect on or write in your journal about what you think is the richest blessing He could give you. Then thank Him for it.

MORE SCRIPTURE FOR STUDY:
Isaiah 33:6; Matthew 13:44;
Luke 12:32-34; Colossians 2:2-3

Whiteness

They will walk with me, dressed in white, for they are worthy.

REVELATION 3:4b

MY SISTER'S AUGUST garden is full of tall, multicolored phlox. Their shades of purple, blue, and pink paint a picture across her perennial beds that inspires thoughts of Monet's watercolors. The phlox colors are so bright and vibrant you would think they must be the standard by which all other colors are judged.

What really stand out the most—and what my sister says bring repeated compliments—are the glistening white phlox. Your eye is drawn over and over to the whiteness, despite the array of colors surrounding it. It sparkles so much, you would think that my sister is in her garden each day polishing each individual little blossom.

Why are the white phlox more noticeable than those with other colors? Our eyes are naturally drawn to what appears to be the most pristine. We have an innate desire to embrace purity and make it part of our lives.

Isn't that why the Lord compares His forgiveness of our sins to being cleansed pure white? "Though your sins are like scarlet, they shall be white as snow; though they are red as crimson, they shall be like wool" (Isa. 1:18).

What perfect imagery. Though shades of red are beautiful and certainly part of the Lord's created spectrum of color, wouldn't you rather think of your forgiven soul as white rather than red?

As the summer draws to an end, consider the imagery of whiteness around you. Look for it in the high wispy clouds or in a garden with daisy petals or impatiens. Reflect on how your sins are no longer red because of Christ's sacrifice for you. Thanks to Him they are "white as snow."

MORE SCRIPTURE FOR STUDY:
Psalm 51:1-10; Hosea 14:1-2;
Matthew 26:27-28; 1 John 1:9

The Lord Is Loving

Your love, O LORD, reaches to the heavens,
your faithfulness to the skies.

PSALM 36:5

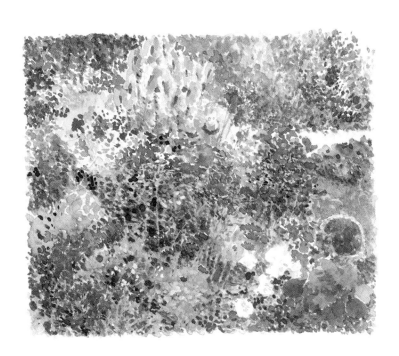

Tender Gardening

Let us not become weary in doing good, for at the proper time
we will reap a harvest if we do not give up.

GALATIANS 6:9

I LOVE TO EAT the produce from my little garden. I'll pop ripe cherry tomatoes in my mouth as I do barn chores. I'll wash a dirt-covered carrot in a watering bucket and eat it unpeeled. I'll shell peas as I'm walking along the garden path and eat the sweet, crisp peas raw.

It still amazes me that what I planted in the spring becomes food that I can eat and be nourished by. Yet my problem is that I love the reaping, but I'm impatient at sowing. Pesky mayflies bug me during spring planting. I find weeding tedious. In my hurry sometimes I'll pull up healthy vegetable plants by accident. I hate the feel of dirt under my nails. I wash my hands five times for every half-hour in the garden. But I cling to the knowledge that eating the vegetables will be worth the discomforts. So I refuse to give up.

My impatient nature, however, spills over into the rest of my life sometimes. Why can't my kids *grow up* and learn to get along? Why can't a needy friend cope for just a few days without calling in a panic? Why can't my husband remember what I just told him yesterday about my schedule today?

Paul reminds us, "Let us not become weary." And "do not give up." It would be easy to allow impatience or frustration with the tending to encourage me to give up on growing the garden.

Do we sometimes bring that same attitude to tending our families? Do we believe that the effort and time we put in now will bring a fruitful, beautiful, and nourishing harvest? Hebrews reminds us of the promise of a hard-won harvest: "No discipline seems pleasant at the time, but painful. Later on, however, it produces a harvest of righteousness and peace for those who have been trained by it" (12:11).

This week practice patience in the tending of your family. Know that you are tilling the fertile ground of their spirits so they can grow strong and deep in their faith. The fruit of your tender, patient sowing will be their ability to nourish others. That's worth getting your hands dirty for!

MORE SCRIPTURE FOR STUDY:
Deuteronomy 16:15; 2 Corinthians 9:6-15;
Galatians 5:22; James 5:7-10

The Humble Sunflower

For to me, to live is Christ and to die is gain.

PHILIPPIANS 1:21

SUNFLOWERS, THE GIANTS of my garden, line a split-rail section of one of our fences. They grow tall and lanky. Their huge, bright yellow blossoms throw shadows across the lawn edge. They add cheer and color while steadily hanging on through rainstorms and winds.

I love their large heads. They're aptly named *sun*flower as each yellow petal reaches out from the center of the blossom like a single ray. But the quality I like most about them is their humility. Their heads are always bowed as if in reverence to their Creator and namesake. (Perhaps *Sonflower* is a better name!) The tallest, most noticeable sunflowers are also the ones whose necks bend the most. It's as if the bigger they grow, the more humble they become.

There's a lesson for us in the sunflowers. The more we take on a demeanor of humility in Christ, the more He can use us in a big way. The apostle Peter wrote of this humility. "Clothe yourselves with humility toward one another, because, 'God opposes the proud but gives grace to the humble.' Humble yourselves, therefore, under God's mighty hand, that he may lift you up in due time" (1 Peter 5:5-6).

Don't you want to be like the sunflowers at full bloom in September? I do. I want my spine to be straight and true to my convictions of growing up toward Christ. I want my head perpetually bowed in honor of His name. I want there to be less of me and more of Him.

Can you feel the Lord's hand ever so gently persuading your neck to bend in humbleness before Him? Will you take a lesson from the sunflowers that show us how to stand tall and straight in God's call, and yet reverently bow in submission? "Therefore stand in awe of God" (Eccl. 5:7b).

MORE SCRIPTURE FOR STUDY:
Proverbs 11:2; Matthew 23:12;
1 Corinthians 15:58; James 3:13-18

Meat Faith

Anyone who lives on milk, being still an infant,
is not acquainted with the teaching about righteousness.
But solid food is for the mature.

HEBREWS 5:13-14

HAVE YOU EVER watched a mother animal start to wean her baby from nursing? It's a normal, natural process in the animal kingdom; yet it can look so heartless. A baby lamb drops to its knees and, little tail wagging, reaches for its mother's udder only to be impatiently kicked away. Or a kitten snuggles next to its mother for a quick drink, and the mother immediately gets up and darts off. The baby is left mewing, wondering where lunch went.

This is what I expected at months four and five when my horse, Galilee, was a foal. But his mother didn't seem interested in weaning him. She allowed him to drink and tug on her well past the normal age of weaning. When he reached eight months, I decided I needed to separate them. But when I returned Galilee's mother to the pasture after a month apart, Galilee tore to her side. He practically knocked her down and stuck his nose under her for a drink. The amazing thing is that she let him! *Shame on her,* I thought. *She just encouraged him to remain a baby.* (Even now, as a twelve-year-old, despite spending numerous lengthy times away, Galilee has an unusually strong bond with his mother.)

Don't we too find ourselves reluctant to be weaned from what I call "milk faith"? Milk faith is when we defiantly say "no" to the Lord's request for obedience. Milk faith is when we act immaturely toward our friends, family, or coworkers by holding grudges or gossiping. Why do we refuse to give up our milk faith? Because it's easy and readily available.

Yet we need to start living on meat faith. We need to ingest God's solid Word and, as the verse above says, live in righteousness. Yes, meat faith is harder to gain because it requires more effort. But when we're mature enough to take in meat, we're mature enough for bigger tasks and more responsibility. Who among us wants to stay a baby, whining at our Provider's feet? I don't. Bring on the steak, Lord!

MORE SCRIPTURE FOR STUDY:
Proverbs 2:1-11; Daniel 12:3; Luke 8:1-15; Ephesians 4:12-16

All-Day Glory

God did not give us the spirit of timidity, but a spirit of power,
of love and of self-discipline.

2 TIMOTHY 1:7

MORNING GLORY VINES climb up the front entrance walls of my barn. Each summer I diligently plant the little torpedo-shaped seeds. As soon as they show a vine, I tack string up the wall for them to climb. By September they have multiple, triangular buds poking out from the vines.

Compared to other flowers that open when the sun hits them, the morning glories open at first light to reveal pale blue and violet blossoms. I try to catch them opening just as I enter the barn to feed the animals. Sometimes I find the buds still tightly furled. At other times, they are already fully open, brave and upright as they face the sun.

The sad thing about morning glories is that they only last for the morning. By the time the midday September sun hits them, they've already started to wilt. The edges curl in, and the whole blossom limply hangs down as if all of its energy has been spent. It's such a contrast to their brilliance just a few hours before.

Aren't we like the morning glories at times? Maybe we start out full of energy and life in the newness of a project or ministry; then we curl up in fear or fatigue once the initial enthusiasm has waned.

The above verse tells us that God has not given us the "spirit of timidity." If God doesn't give us timidity, where does it come from? Guess. Ourselves. The enemy of our souls—Satan. What *does* God give us? Power, love, and self-discipline—power to stand firm in our convictions, love for the task at hand and the people involved, and self-discipline to keep going when discouragement threatens. Those certainly will boost flagging enthusiasm.

Although I love morning glories, I'd rather reflect God's glory all day. How about you?

MORE SCRIPTURE FOR STUDY:
Psalm 90:12; 2 Corinthians 4:16;
2 Thessalonians 2:13-17; 1 Peter 4:7-11

Making Allowances

We have different gifts, according to the grace given us. If a man's
gift is prophesying, let him use it in proportion to his faith.
If it is serving, let him serve; if it is teaching, let him teach;
if it is encouraging, let him encourage; if it is contributing to
the needs of others, let him give generously; if it is leadership,
let him govern diligently; if it is showing mercy,
let him do it cheerfully.

ROMANS 12:6-8

DIVERSITY IS THE artwork of a well-planned perennial garden. Ideally there should be flowering plants during each month of the growing season. In New England that means from late April through October. It wouldn't make sense to have all of the plants bloom only in the month of June. Also it would not make sense to have the same kinds of plants throughout the garden. Varying heights of plants, blossom sizes and colors, and different greens all add to the beauty of a garden.

The members of the body of Christ are like a garden. In the garden of life with other Christians, don't we often presume that everyone should be about the same? Perhaps we have biases about what clothing people should wear to church. Perhaps we judge those who worship differently than we do. Maybe we assume that all children should go to Sunday school.

Most notably we sometimes feel impatience when other people's gifts are different from ours or when they don't do what we think they should do. We mutter, "Why can't Stacey work on the missions committee? She has the time." But maybe Stacey's gift isn't a good fit for this area. What good would she do on a committee where she has trouble ministering effectively?

The above passage reminds us to allow people to minister in the areas where they are gifted and release them from other areas. Freedom to serve is granted through the words "let him." Let him, affirm him, and nurture him in those areas where God has equipped him (or her).

Just as variety means beauty in our gardens, so it is in our churches. Allow a rose to stay a rose in your garden. In church encourage your friends to be who God made them to be. Let's *let* them.

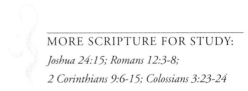

MORE SCRIPTURE FOR STUDY:
Joshua 24:15; Romans 12:3-8;
2 Corinthians 9:6-15; Colossians 3:23-24

Listen Carefully

The sheep listen to his voice. . . . He goes on ahead of them,
and his sheep follow him because they know his voice.

JOHN 10:3-4

FIVE DAYS AFTER getting a new horse, I let him go out on the fields with two of our other horses. He'd had a chance to meet the others, but hadn't really formed the herd mentality with them yet.

After they grazed for several hours, I stood on the deck of my home and looked out across the valley to the fields. I whistled, clapped my hands, and called each horse by name, asking him or her to come back to the barn. Before the first whistle even died in the air, Galilee, who's been with me from his moment of birth, lifted his head and immediately broke into a canter across the field to come home. My daughter's pony followed shortly behind. But the new horse watched the other horses run toward the barn. He seemed unconcerned, because he didn't consider them part of his herd. So he promptly went back to eating. Apparently he was not impressed with my call or the draw of the barn. I had to fetch a lead rope and walk down the valley and up the next hillside to retrieve him.

It's not that the new horse had run away from me or was disobedient. He just didn't recognize my voice when I called. He hadn't learned that good things (i.e., grain and carrots) were associated with my voice.

Do you recognize God's voice when He calls you? Do you have a close enough relationship with Him to hear His call? Maybe He calls you with a whisper to your heart that nudges you to do something. Or maybe you hear Him best through reading Scripture, because His Word at times is very personal. Perhaps you hear His voice the most when you are in the midst of His creation.

"The LORD longs to be gracious to you" (Isa. 30:18). I've learned that good things are associated with recognizing and responding to the Lord's voice. What good things? Perhaps blessings in relationships, in finances, or through others' ministry to us. Jesus said, "He who has ears, let him hear" (Matt. 11:15). Are you listening?

MORE SCRIPTURE FOR STUDY:
Deuteronomy 31:12-13; Psalm 95:7-8;
Ezekiel 34:22-31; John 5:24-27

In Common

The remaining area ... will be used for the common use of the city,
for houses and for pastureland.

EZEKIEL 48:15

ONE DAY WHILE walking across the vast open grass of Boston Common, I thought about all of the towns across New England that have a "common" in or near the center of town. The commons are open spaces of grassy flats, frequently with a stream or pond, and edged all around by the town itself—stores, roads, and houses. As in the adage "all roads lead to Rome," all of the old roads in New England towns led to the common.

Kicking along an acorn on one of the sidewalks that run through Boston Common, I thought about the concept of "common" land. Historically the land was set aside for the city dwellers who kept livestock as part of their commerce. The horses that trudged through the streets each day were turned out on the common land at night along with the cows belonging to the merchants. Undoubtedly the users of the common land also worked together to build the fences and rotate the herds.

Today common land plots are giant parks for playing, walking, or relaxing. This is a good use of beautiful land. But what's been lost? The idea of shared property. We want ownership, don't we? We post signs threatening lawsuits if people trespass. We lock our doors. We don't trust other people.

Is there a way we could share something in common in the twenty-first century? Most people certainly don't have livestock needing shared ground for grazing. But there is a sense in which we have potential common ground in our homes. First Peter 4:9 says, "Offer hospitality to one another without grumbling." The Lord has given you your home. Pray about how to use it as a place for friends to gather to be spiritually fed.

MORE SCRIPTURE FOR STUDY:
Joshua 24:15; Luke 19:1-10; Acts 2:42-47;
Romans 12:9-13

A Daily Reminder

This very night, before the rooster crows,
you will disown me three times.

MATTHEW 26:34

THE FIRST YEAR we raised chickens for meat, the company from which we ordered the birds included two "exotic" chickens in the flock of seventy-five. We curiously watched these birds grow—one black and white, the other downy white—knowing they weren't meat birds, but wondering what they were.

Our wondering stopped when the black and white one cackled out an adolescent crow at four months old. Within a few days of putting up with this noise, we knew why people in the past had asked us, "Can't we *please* give you our rooster?"

His voice improved, my ears adjusted, and the children affectionately named him Farley. He was named after my daughter's favorite author, Walter Farley. (The white one is named Waltress.)

Farley is a character. He "buck-bucks" about with Waltress, but when he hears a noise—human, dog, or car—he announces his presence with powerful clarity. He rarely crows just once. He usually gives a succession of crows and clucks as he struts and plumes his feathers.

As much as his antics amuse me, when I hear him around dusk as he sends out his last call from the barn, I often think of Jesus' words to Peter. Those heart-wrenching words foretold Peter's betrayal: "Before the rooster crows, you will disown me three times." Peter was affronted, as I would have been too. "Even if I have to die with you, I will never disown you," he declared (26:35).

Yet when I hear Farley issuing his evening proclamation, I wonder if and how, over the day, I too have denied my Christ three times. Did I fail to bear witness of Him through my actions or thoughts? Did I ignore the Holy Spirit's prodding? Did I speak unnecessarily harshly to my children or husband? In each way I've denied my Lord.

I don't want to tune out that final crow of the evening on our farm. I need it as a daily reminder to ask the Lord to forgive me for denying Him in big and small ways. When the sun rises the next morning and I hear Farley greeting the day, I know that, like Peter, I've been forgiven and granted another day to try again.

MORE SCRIPTURE FOR STUDY:
Matthew 26:31-35, 69-75; John 21:1-19;
2 Timothy 2:13

Only One Gate

*"I am the gate; whoever enters through me will be saved.
He will come in and go out, and find pasture."*

JOHN 10:9

THE WINTER PADDOCKS for my horses stand close to the barn and are divided into small lots by wood fencing. A series of metal gates open and close between the paddocks, to create larger spaces or smaller spaces.

In the summer and early fall months, however, there is one particular gate that the horses want to see open—the gate leading to the fields of lush grass and clover. None of the other gates open to those fields.

One would think that the horses would figure that out pretty quickly, as they are generally intelligent creatures who like to eat. But even after twelve years, Galilee still runs to a different part of the fence first and impatiently paws it with his front hoof, asking to go to the fields that way. I think it's probably because he can see the fields from that spot and doesn't understand why he can't go through the fence there. But he has to use the prepared gate—no other way will work.

After a while he gets sick of his own game and trots up one short hill, through a gate, and down another hill to go through the real gate to the fields. Then he breaks into a pounding gallop as he tries to catch up with the other horses that have gone ahead of him. I shake my head with wonder at his silly habit.

Jesus says that He is the one true gate by which we all need to pass into heaven. His words imply that there are tempting gates that we rattle impatiently all around us. Like my horse, people may be able to visualize where they want to go—heaven. But Christ says that the only route to the final safe pasture of heaven is through Him as the gate.

I'm glad He prepared a gate for me to be able to enter into His presence. Like the psalmist, I can proclaim, "Open the gates of righteousness; I will enter and give thanks to the LORD" (Ps. 118:19). Aren't you also grateful to have the assurance that we're through that narrow gate and on our way to the safe pasture of heaven?

MORE SCRIPTURE FOR STUDY:
Psalm 100:4-5; Isaiah 62:10;
Matthew 7:13-14; John 14:1-7

Volumes of Praise

Jesus did many other things as well. If every one of them were written down, I suppose that even the whole world would not have room for the books that would be written.

JOHN 21:25

I LOVE BOOKS. (Maybe that's why I write them.) Mysteries, devotionals, Christian living, suspense, biographies, children's books, poetry, writing, family and marriage books—you name it, I probably like it. Consequently, books pile up on the living room coffee table, a stack teeters by the side of my bed, and there are layers of them in my office—not necessarily on shelves either.

I chuckle at the apostle John's musing above about there not being enough room in the world for the volumes of books required to document all of Jesus' life and activities. And I thought *I* had a lot of books! But John's contemplation also makes me feel shortchanged almost, as if something important could be missing from the Bible. Of course I know that's not true, because the Word of the Lord is complete in its inspiration and content. Yet I still yearn to *know*

Jesus and feel dismayed to think that there is more to be told than what the Bible has recorded. Don't you want to know what those volumes would say?

It was out of character for the apostles to be extravagant in the expression of their thoughts. Yet those words seem to say so much about how John felt concerning the Lord. John speculated that the earth would run out of space before Jesus' story could be told in full. John's words speak his admiration, honor, and praise. What a testimony to the impact of Jesus' life!

We can't add to the words of the Bible, but we can add our testimony of what Christ has done in our lives. What about writing your own private volume of what the Lord has done for you? Think about how He's blessed you or how He has touched others through you. Let's take John's thought as a challenge. Let's fill the earth with testimonies of Christ's ministry.

MORE SCRIPTURE FOR STUDY:
Psalms 19:14; 45:1; Isaiah 50:4;
Matthew 24:14

Raising Righteousness

Peacemakers who sow in peace raise a harvest of righteousness.

JAMES 3:18

THE PHRASE "a harvest of righteousness" brings a beautiful image to mind: a vast wheat field in the Midwest. Heady golden stalks sway in the breeze under a blue, blue sky. When gently rubbed, the crisp tops give way to grains of wheat to be used as nourishing food. The field is so vivid and inviting in my mind's eye that I imagine myself sitting between the stalks, listening to the gentle hum and brush of the wheat against itself.

I'm attempting to raise a harvest of righteousness in my home. I want the tranquillity I imagine from the giant wheat field to penetrate my home's atmosphere. But that goal is hard to attain when what I am trying to harvest as the Lord's (my children) won't practice peace in the way the above verse recommends.

Upon the rare occasion when my children fight—really fight—the roar of their bickering voices sounds like a growling tractor. The revving of their engines makes me feel that my desired tranquil harvest of righteousness is in danger of being mowed down.

But then I think about what I want to model as I try to sow peace aplenty to raise that hoped-for righteousness. When I intervene in their argument, am I sowing impatience and a rigid heart, or am I sowing graciousness and forgiveness?

James 3:17 says, "The wisdom that comes from heaven is first of all pure; then peace-loving, considerate, submissive, full of mercy and good fruit, impartial and sincere." Isn't this what we want to sow within and model to our children—a pure tongue when we correct them, a kind and merciful heart, and a sincere ear to hear both sides of the story?

I find that when I sow peace within my children during their moments of bickering, they respond more peacefully. My prayer is that they will grow in righteousness as I continue to spread more peace between them.

What's the added benefit when we sow peace? We grow in righteousness when we are able to keep a peaceful attitude. Will you work this week to promote peace among those you love?

MORE SCRIPTURE FOR STUDY:
Psalm 133; Proverbs 19:11;
1 Corinthians 13:1-9, 13; James 5:16

We Are Victorious!

*Thanks be to God! He gives us the victory through our
Lord Jesus Christ.*

1 CORINTHIANS 15:57

NEW HAMPSHIRE'S NICKNAME IS "The Granite State." Beautiful granite is mined from quarries across the state. If only the rocks "grew" just in the quarries. Instead, the rocks are *everywhere* in New Hampshire!

We are repeatedly reminded that we live in the granite state every time we dig holes for fence posts. It seems as if the land itself mocks us. It's guaranteed that within the first three thrusts of the posthole digger, a sharp "ping" is heard. The duller the "ping," the bigger the rock. Such was the case when Peter decided to replace a corner fence post that had not been grounded deep enough.

After a few swipes with the digger and a shovel, he heard the dreaded sound. Deciding to dig around the rock to move it, he found the hole becoming increasingly wider. (You might wonder, *Why not dig a different hole for the post?* To change the location of the corner post would have meant moving the entire fence line.) Finally, all of the edges were exposed, but that was only half the problem. How could he now remove the close to 500-pound boulder he had discovered? Between the tractor, a chain, a come-along winch, brute strength, and his family as a cheering squad, the rock finally budged up over the lip of the hole and slid to the side. Over four hours had gone by. Peter was muddy and bruised—all for one fence post. But the victory over the rock-producing ground felt sweet. We all clapped and cheered.

My mind started singing the song, "Victory in Jesus." That moment did feel like a huge battle won. Aren't you glad we will *always* have victory in Jesus' name? "For everyone born of God overcomes the world. This is the victory that has overcome the world, even our faith. Who is it that overcomes the world? Only he who believes that Jesus is the Son of God" (1 John 5:4-5). His victory is worth fighting for, don't you think?

MORE SCRIPTURE FOR STUDY:
2 Samuel 7:18—8:14; Psalms 21:1-7; 60:12

Immortal, Invisible, God Only Wise

Immortal, invisible, God only wise,
In light inaccessible hid from our eyes,
Most blessed, most glorious, the Ancient of Days,
Almighty, victorious, Thy great name we praise.

Unresting, unhasting, and silent as light,
Nor wanting, nor wasting, Thou rulest in might;
Thy justice, like mountains, high soaring above
Thy clouds, which are fountains of goodness and love.

To all, life Thou givest, to both great and small;
In all life Thou livest, the true life of all;
We blossom and flourish as leaves on the tree,
And wither and perish—but naught changeth Thee.

Great Father of glory, pure Father of light,
Thine angels adore Thee, all veiling their sight;
All praise we would render—O help us to see
'Tis only the splendor of light hideth Thee!

A NATIVE NEW ENGLANDER, Elizabeth Hoekstra lives on a farm in southern New Hampshire with her husband, Peter, and their two children. She holds an R.N. degree, with a concentration in psychology and maternal health, and has worked in both hospital and community health settings. Currently she manages Direct Path Ministries, which encourages women and families to form deeper interpersonal relationships under the lordship of Jesus Christ. Elizabeth also gardens, shows her horse Galilee, and enjoys skiing, boating, kayaking, biking, and hiking with her family.

Other Crossway books by Elizabeth M. Hoekstra

Keeping Your Family Close When Frequent Travel Pulls You Apart

Just for Girls

Just for Moms

A Season of Gladness

A Season of Grace

A Season of Stillness

With Mary Bradford

Chronic Kids, Constant Hope

MARLENE McLOUGHLIN WAS BORN IN BUFFALO, NEW YORK, and grew up in southern California. She received a degree in art history from Barnard College in New York City and a degree in drawing "with high distinction" from California College of Arts and Crafts.

In 1998 she went to Rome to work on her book *Road to Rome* (Chronicle Books) and decided to stay because of the beauty of the landscape and because dogs are allowed almost everywhere. She lives with Kiddo, a tortoise shell cat, and Barely, a German-Italian shepherd mix … both pets are bilingual!

Marlene works from home on projects that vary from logo design to wall paintings. Her internationally award-winning books include: *Diane Seed's Rome for All Seasons, Across the Aegean,* and *The Passionate Observer.* Her clients include Linda Ronstadt, Williams-Sonoma, Ten Speed Press, and HarperCollins.

The typeface for this book is Adobe Garamond, originally designed by Claude Garamond in 1532. His oldstyle designs, based on the Aldine model, were the typefaces of choice in the composing rooms of printers well into the 18th century. In 1989 Robert Slimbach modified the design of this typeface slightly for Adobe, and it remains a favorite for book designers today.

The script used throughout is Escrita, a three weight, hand-drawn face designed by Mário Feliciano for T-26 in 1997.

The interior for this series was set by Joe Rosewell and Rose Graham.